Ossian

Legends

as told by

James MacPherson

Mudborn Press

2014

Ossian Legends © 2014 Mudborn Press

ISBN 978-0-930012-50-2

LITERARY FICTION

Family Secret, Last American Housewife, Period Pieces, Eleanore Hill
Aurora Leigh, E.B. Browning   Hadji Murad, Tolstoy   **The Basement,**
Newborn **The First Detective**. Poe   **Matilda,** Jewell Shelley

SPECULATIVE FICTION

Frankenstein, Mary Shelley   **The Martian Testament,** Sasha Newborn

HISTORY

Mitos y Leyendas/Myths and Legends of Mexico. Bilingual
Beechers Through the 19th Century   Uncle Tom's Cabin, H. B. Stowe

SCHOOLING

Don't Panic: Procrastinator's Guide to Writing an Effective Term Paper
First Person Intense   Italian for Opera Lovers
French for Food Lovers Doctorese for the imPatient

SCHOOLING

Ghazals of Ghalib   Gandhi on the *Bhagavad Gita*
Gospel According to Tolstoy Everlasting Gospel, William Blake

LOVE

Dante & His Circle. Love sonnets   **Vita Nuova   Sappho**

STAGING SHAKESPEARE

DIRECTOR'S PLAYBOOK SERIES: Hamlet   Merchant of Venice
Twelfth Night   Taming of the Shrew   Midsummer Night's Dream
Romeo and Lydiat As You Like It Richard III Henry V Much Ado About
Nothing Macbeth Othello Julius Caesar King Lear Antony and Cleopatra

7 Plays with Transgender Characters   Falstaff: 4 Plays Venus and
Adonis

TEACHERS ONLY

(*Q & A, glossaries, critical comments*)
Areopagitica, John Milton   **Apology of Socrates, & Crito,** Plato
Leaves of Grass, Walt Whitman   **Sappho, The Poems**

1

Shilric and Vinvela

Vinvela. My love is a son of the hill.
He pursues the flying deer.
His grey dogs are panting
around him; his bow-string sounds in
the wind. Whether by the fount of
the rock, or by the stream of the
mountain you lie; when the rushes are
nodding with the wind, and the mist
is flying over you, let me approach
my love unperceived, and see him
from the rock. Lovely I saw you
first by the aged oak; you were returning
tall from the chase; the fairest
among your friends.

Shilric. What voice is that I hear? that
voice like the summer-wind.—I sit
not by the nodding rushes; I hear not
the fount of the rock. Afar, Vinvela,
afar I go to the wars of Fingal. My
dogs attend me no more. No more

I tread the hill. No more from on
high I see you, fair-moving by the
stream of the plain; bright as the
bow of heaven; as the moon on the
western wave.

Vinvela. Then you are gone, O Shilric!
and I am alone on the hill. The
deer are seen on the brow; void of
fear they graze along. No more they
dread the wind; no more the rustling
tree. The hunter is far removed;
he is in the field of graves. Strangers!
Sons of the waves! Spare my
lovely Shilric.

Shilric. If fall I must in the field, raise high
my grave, Vinvela. Grey stones, and
heaped-up earth, shall murk me to future
times. When the hunter shall sit by
the mound, and produce his food at
noon, "some warrior rests here," he
will say; and my fame shall live in his
praise. Remember me, Vinvela, when
low on earth I lie!

Vinvela. Yes!—I will remember you—indeed
my Shilric will fall. What shall I do,
my love! when you are gone forever?
Through these hills I will go at noon: I
will go through the silent heath. There
I will see where often you sat returning
from the chase. Indeed, my Shilric
will fall; but I will remember him.

2

I sit by the mossy fountain; on the top of the hill of winds. One tree is rustling above me. Dark waves roll over the heath. The lake is troubled below. The deer descend from the hill. No hunter at a distance is seen; no whistling cow-herd is nigh. It is mid-day: but all is silent. Sad are my thoughts as I sit alone. Did you but appear, O my love, a wanderer on the heath! your hair floating on the wind behind you; your bosom heaving on the sight; your eyes full of tears for your friends, whom the mist of the hill had concealed! You I would comfort, my love, and bring you to your father's house.

But is it she that there appears, like a beam of light on the heath? Bright as the moon in autumn, as the sun in a summer-storm?—She speaks: but how weak her voice! like the breeze in the reeds of the pool. Hark!

Return you safe from the war?
"Where are your friends, my love? I
heard of your death on the hill; I heard
and mourned you, Shilric!"

Yes, my fair, I return; but I alone
of my race. You shall see them no
more: their graves I raised on the plain.
But why are you on the desert hill?
Why on the heath, alone?

Alone I am, O Shilric! Alone in the
winter-house. With grief for you I
expired. Shilric, I am pale in the tomb.

She fleets, she sails away; as grey
mist before the wind!—And will you
not stay, my love? Stay and behold
my tears? Fair you appear, my love!
Fair you were, when alive!

By the mossy fountain I will sit; on
the top of the hill of winds. When
mid-day is silent around, converse, O
my love, with me! come on the wings
of the gale! on the blast of the mountain,
come! Let me hear your voice, as
you pass, when mid-day is silent around.

3

Evening is grey on the hills. The
north wind resounds through the
woods. White clouds rise on the sky: the
trembling snow descends. The river howls
afar, along its winding course. Sad,
by a hollow rock, the grey-haired Carryl
sat. Dry fern waves over his head; his
seat is in an aged birch. Clear to the
roaring winds he lifts his voice of woe.

Tossed on the wavy ocean is he,
the hope of the isles; Malcolm, the
support of the poor; foe to the proud
in arms! Why have you left us behind?
Why live we to mourn your fate? We
might have heard, with you, the voice
of the deep; have seen the oozy rock.

Sad on the sea-beat shore your spouse
looks for your return. The time of
your promise is come; the night is gathering
around. But no white sail is
on the sea; no voice is heard except
the blustering winds. Low is the soul
of the war! Wet are the locks of youth!
By the foot of some rock you lie;

washed by the waves as they come.
Why, you winds, did you bear him on
the desert rock? Why, you waves, did
you roll over him?

But, Oh! what voice is that?
Who rides on that meteor of fire! Green
are his airy limbs. It is he! It is the
ghost of Malcolm!—Rest, lovely soul,
rest on the rock; and let me hear your
voice!—He is gone, like a dream of
the night. I see him through the trees.
Daughter of Reynold! He is gone.
Your spouse shall return no more. No
more shall his hounds come from the
hill, forerunners of their master. No
more from the distant rock shall his
voice greet your ear. Silent is he in
the deep, unhappy daughter of Reynold!

I will sit by the stream of the plain.
You rocks! hang over my head. Hear
my voice, you trees! as you bend on the
shaggy hill. My voice shall preserve
the praise of him, the hope of the isles.

4

Connal and Crimora

Crimora. Who comes from the hill, like
a cloud tinged with the beam
of the west? Whose voice is that, loud
as the wind, but pleasant as the harp of
Carryl? It is my love in the light of
steel; but sad is his darkened brow.
Live the mighty race of Fingal? or
what disturbs my Connal?

Connal. They live. I saw them return from
the chase, like a stream of light. The
sun was on their shields: In a line they
descended the hill. Loud is the voice of
the youth; the war, my love, is near.
Tomorrow the enormous Dargo comes
to try the force of our race. The race of
Fingal he defies; the race of battle and wounds.

Crimora. Connal, I saw his sails like grey mist
on the sable wave. They came to land.
Connnal, many are the warriors of Dargo!

Connal. Bring me your father's shield; the iron shield of Rinval; that shield like the full moon when it is darkened in the sky.

Crimora. That shield I bring, O Connal; but it did not defend my father. By the spear of Gauror he fell. You may fall, O Connal!

Connal. Fall indeed I may: But raise my tomb, Crimora. Some stones, a mound of earth, shall keep my memory. Though fair you are, my love, as the light; more pleasant than the gale of the hill; yet I will not stay. Raise my tomb, Crimora.

Crimora. Then give me those arms of light; that sword, and that spear of steel. I shall meet Dargo with you, and aid my lovely Connal. Farewell, you rocks of Ardven! You deer! And you streams of the hill!—We shall return no more. Our tombs are distant far.

5

Autumn is dark on the mountains;
grey mist rests on the hills. The
whirlwind is heard on the heath. Dark
rolls the river through the narrow plain.
A tree stands alone on the hill, and
marks the grave of Connal. The leaves
whirl round with the wind, and strew
the grave of the dead. At times are
seen here the ghosts of the deceased,
when the musing hunter alone stalks
slowly over the heath.

Who can reach the source of your
race, O Connal? and who recount your
Fathers? Your family grew like an oak
on the mountain, which meet the
wind with its lofty head. But now it
is torn from the earth. Who shall supply
the place of Connal?

Here was the din of arms; and
here the groans of the dying. Mournful
are the wars of Fingal! O Connal!
It was here you did fall. Your arm
was like a storm; your sword, a beam
of the sky; your height, a rock on the

plain; your eyes, a furnace of fire.
Louder than a storm was your voice,
when you confounded the field. Warriors
fell by your sword, as the thistle by
the staff of a boy.

Dargo the mighty came on, like a
cloud of thunder. His brows were contracted
and dark. His eyes like two
caves in a rock. Bright rose their
swords on each side; dire was the clang
of their steel.

The daughter of Rinval was near;
Crimora, bright in the armor of man;
her hair loose behind, her bow in her
hand. She followed the youth to the
war, Connal her much beloved. She
drew the string on Dargo; but, erring,
pierced her Connal. He falls like an
oak on the plain; like a rock from the
shaggy hill. What shall she do, hapless
maid!—He bleeds; her Connal dies.
All the night long she cries, and all the
day, O Connal, my love, and my
friend! With grief the sad mourner died.

Earth here enclose the loveliest
pair on the hill. The grass grows between
the stones of their tomb; I sit in
the mournful shade. The wind sighs
through the grass; and their memory
rushes on my mind. Undisturbed you
now sleep together; in the tomb of the
mountain you rest alone.

6

Son of the noble Fingal, Ossian,
Prince of men! what tears run down
the cheeks of age? What shades your
mighty soul?

Memory, son of Alpin, memory
wounds the aged. Of former times are
my thoughts; my thoughts are of the
noble Fingal. The race of the king return
into my mind, and wound me with
remembrance.

One day, returned from the sport of
the mountains, from pursuing the sons
of the hill, we covered this heath with
our youth. Fingal the mighty was here,
and Oscur, my son, great in war. Fair
on our sight from the sea, at once, a
virgin came. Her breast was like the
snow of one night. Her cheek like the
bud of the rose. Mild was her blue
rolling eye: but sorrow was big in her heart.

"Fingal renowned in war!" she cries,
"Sons of the king, preserve me!" "Speak, secure,"
replies the king, "Daughter of beauty,

speak: our ear is open to all: our
swords redress the injured." "I fly from
Ullin," she cries, "from Ullin famous in
war. I fly from the embrace of him
who would debase my blood. Cremor,
the friend of men, was my father; Cremor
the Prince of Inverne."

Fingal's younger sons arose; Carryl
expert in the bow; Fillan beloved of
the fair; and Fergus first in the race.
—"Who from the farthest Lochlyn?
Who to the seas of Molochasquir? Who
dares hurt the maid whom the sons of
Fingal guard? Daughter of beauty, rest
secure; rest in peace, you fairest of women."

Far in the blue distance of the deep,
some spot appeared like the back of the
ridge-wave. But soon the ship increased
on our sight. The hand of Ullin drew
her to land. The mountains trembled
as he moved. The hills shook at his
steps. Dire rattled his armor around
him. Death and destruction were in his
eyes. His stature like the roe of Morven.
He moved in the lightning of steel.

Our warriors fell before him,
like the field before the reapers. Fingal's
three sons he bound. He plunged
his sword into the fair-one's breast.
She fell as a wreath of snow before the
sun in spring. Her bosom heaved in

death; her soul came forth in blood.
Oscur my son came down; the
mighty in battle descended. His armor
rattled as thunder; and the lightning of
his eyes was terrible. There, was the
clashing of swords; there, was the voice
of steel. They struck and they thrust;
they dug for death with their swords.
But death was distant far, and delayed
to come. The sun began to decline;
and the cow-herd thought of home.
Then Oscur's keen steel found the heart
of Ullin. He fell like a mountain-oak
covered over with glittering frost: He
shone like a rock on the plain.—Here
the daughter of beauty lies; and
here the bravest of men. Here one
day ended the fair and the valiant.
Here rest the pursuer and the pursued.

Son of Alpin! the woes of the aged
are many: their tears are for the past.
This raised my sorrow, warrior; memory
awaked my grief. Oscur my
son was brave; but Oscur is now no
more. You have heard my grief, O
son of Alpin; forgive the tears of the aged.

7

Why open you afresh the spring of
my grief, O son of Alpin, inquiring
how Oscur fell? My eyes are blind with
tears; but memory beams on my heart.
How can I relate the mournful death of
the head of the people! Prince of the
warriors, Oscur my son, shall I see you
no more!

He fell as the moon in a storm; as
the sun from the midst of his course,
when clouds rise from the waste of the
waves, when the blackness of the storm
enwraps the rocks of Ardannider. I, like
an ancient oak on Morven, I molder
alone in my place. The blast has lopped
my branches away; and I tremble
at the wings of the north. Prince of
the warriors, Oscur my son! shall I see
you no more!

Dermid and Oscur were one: They
reaped the battle together. Their
friendship was strong as their steel; and
death walked between them to the field.

They came on the foe like two rocks
falling from the brows of Ardven. Their
swords were stained with the blood of
the valiant: warriors fainted at their
names. Who was a match for Oscur,
but Dermid? and who for Dermid, but
Oscur?

They killed mighty Dargo in the
field; Dargo before invincible. His
daughter was fair as the morn; mild
as the beam of night. Her eyes, like
two stars in a shower: her breath, the
gale of spring: her breasts, as the
new fallen snow floating on the moving heath.
The warriors saw her, and loved; their
souls were fixed on the maid. Each
loved her, as his fame; each must
possess her or die. But her soul was fixed
on Oscur; my son was the youth of
her love. She forgot the blood of her
father; and loved the hand that slew him.

"Son of Ossian," said Dermid, "I love;
O Oscur, I love this maid. But her
soul cleaves unto you; and nothing
can heal Dermid. Here, pierce this
bosom, Oscur; relieve me, my friend,
with your sword."

"My sword, son of Morny, shall never
be stained with the blood of Dermid."

"Who then is worthy to slay me, O
Oscur son of Ossian? Let not my life
pass away unknown. Let none but Oscur
slay me. Send me with honor to
the grave, and let my death be renowned.
Dermid, make use of your sword;
son of Moray, wield your steel. Would
that I fell with you! That my death
came from the hand of Dermid!"

They fought by the brook of the
mountain; by the streams of Branno.
Blood tinged the silvery stream, and
curdled round the mossy stones. Dermid
the graceful fell; fell, and smiled in death.

"And fall you, son of Morny;
fall, you by Oscur's hand! Dermid
invincible in war, thus do I see you fall!"
—He went, and returned to the maid
whom he loved; returned, but she perceived
his grief.

"Why that gloom, son of Ossian?
What shades your mighty soul?"

"Though once renowned for the bow,
O maid, I have lost my fame. Fixed on
a tree by the brook of the hill, is the
shield of Gormur the brave, whom in
battle I slew. I have wasted the day
in vain, nor could my arrow pierce it."

"Let me try, son Ossian, the skill
of Dargo's daughter. My hands were
taught the bow: my father delighted in
my skill."

She went. He stood behind the
shield. Her arrow flew and pierced his breast.

"Blessed be that hand of snow; and
blessed your bow of yew! I fall resolved
on death: and who but the daughter of
Dargo was worthy to slay me? Lay me
in the earth, my fair one; lay me by
the side of Dermid."

"Oscur! I have the blood, the soul
of the mighty Dargo. Well pleased I
can meet death. My sorrow I can end
thus."—She pierced her white bosom
with steel. She fell; she trembled; and died.

By the brook of the hill their graves
are laid; a birch's unequal shade covers
their tomb. Often on their green earthen
tombs the branchy sons of the mountain
feed, when mid-day is all in flames,
and silence is over all the hills.

8

By the side of a rock on the hill, beneath
the aged trees, old Ossian
sat on the moss; the last of the race of
Fingal. Sightless are his aged eyes;
his beard is waving in the wind. Dull
through the leafless trees he heard the
voice of the north. Sorrow revived in
his soul: he began and lamented the
dead.

How have you fallen like an oak,
with all your branches round you! Where
is Fingal the King? where is Oscur my
son? where are all my race? Alas! in
the earth they lie. I feel their tombs
with my hands. I hear the river below
murmuring hoarsely over the stones.
What do you, O river, to me? You
bring back the memory of the past.

The race of Fingal stood on your
banks, like a wood in a fertile soil.
Keen were their spears of steel. Hardy
was he who dared to encounter their
rage. Fillan the great was there. You,

Oscur were there, my son! Fingal himself
was there, strong in the grey locks
of years. Full rose his sinewy limbs;
and wide his shoulders spread. The
unhappy met with his arm, when the
pride of his wrath arose.

The son of Morny came; Gaul, the
tallest of men. He stood on the hill like
an oak; his voice was like the streams of
the hill. "Why reign alone," he cries,
"the son of the mighty Corval? Fingal is
not strong to save: he is no support for
the people. I am strong as a storm in
the ocean; as a whirlwind on the hill.
Yield, son of Corval; Fingal, yield to me."

Oscur stood forth to meet him;
my son would meet the foe. But Fingal
came in his strength, and smiled at
the vaunter's boast. They threw their
arms round each other; they struggled
on the plain. The earth is plowed with
their heels. Their bones crack as the boat
on the ocean, when it leaps from wave to
wave. Long did they toil; with night,
they fell on the sounding plain; as two
oaks, with their branches mingled, fall
crashing from the hill. The tall son
of Morny is bound; the aged overcame.

Fair with her locks of gold, her
smooth neck, and her breasts of snow;
fair, as the spirits of the hill when at

silent noon they glide along the heath;
fair, as the rainbow of heaven; came
Minvane the maid. "Fingal!" She softly
said, "Loose me my brother Gaul.
Loose me the hope of my race, the terror
of all but Fingal." "Can I," replies the
King, "Can I deny the lovely daughter
of the hill? Take your brother, O Minvane,
you fairer than the snow of the north!"

Such, Fingal! were your words; but
your words I hear no more. Sightless
I sit by your tomb. I hear the wind in
the wood; but no more I hear my
friends. The cry of the hunter is over.
The voice of war is ceased.

9

You ask, fair daughter of the
isles! whose memory is preserved
in these tombs? The memory of Ronnan
the bold, and Connan the chief of
men; and of her, the fairest of maids,
Rivine the lovely and the good. The
wing of time is laden with care. Every
moment has woes of its own. Why
seek we our grief from afar? or give our
tears to those of other times? But you
commanded, and I obey, O fair daughter
of the isles!

Conar was mighty in war. Caul
was the friend of strangers. His gates
were open to all; midnight darkened
not on his barred door. Both lived upon
the sons of the mountains. Their bow
was the support of the poor.

Connan was the image of Conar's
soul. Caul was renewed in Ronnan his
son. Rivine the daughter of Conar was
the love of Ronnan; her brother Connan
was his friend. She was fair as the
harvest-moon setting in the seas of

Molochasquir. Her soul was settled on
Ronnan; the youth was the dream of her nights.

"Rivine, my love!" says Ronnan, "I go
to my king in Norway. A year and
a day shall bring me back. Will you
be true to Ronnan?"

"Ronnan! a year and a day I will
spend in sorrow. Ronnan, behave like
a man, and my soul shall exult in your
valor." "Connan my friend," says Ronnan,
"Will you preserve Rivine your sister?
Durstan is in love with the maid;
and soon shall the sea bring the stranger
to our coast."

"Ronnan, I will defend: Do you
securely go."—He went. He returned
on his day. But Durstan returned
before him.

"Give me your daughter, Conar," says
Durstan, "or fear and feel my power."

"He who dares attempt my sister," says
Connan, "must meet this edge of steel.
Unerring in battle is my arm: my
sword, as the lightning of heaven."

Ronnan the warrior came; and
much he threatened Durstan.

"But," says Euran the servant of
gold, "Ronnan! By the gate of the north
shall Durstan this night carry your fair one
away." "Accursed," answers Ronnan, "be this arm
if death meet him not there."

"Connan!" says Euran, "this night
shall the stranger carry your sister away."
"My sword shall meet him," replies Connan,
"and he shall lie low on earth."

The friends met by night, and they
fought. Blood and sweat ran down
their limbs as water on the mossy rock.
Connan falls; and cries, "O Durstan,
be favorable to Rivine!"— "And is it my
friend," cries Ronnan, "I have slain? O
Connan! I knew you not."

He went, and he fought with Durstan.
Day began to rise on the combat,
when fainting they fell, and expired.
Rivine came out with the morn;
and—"O what detains my Ronnan!"
—She saw him lying pale in his blood;
and her brother lying pale by his side.

What could she say: what could she
do? her complaints were many and vain.
She opened this grave for the warriors;
and fell into it herself, before it
was closed; like the sun snatched away
in a storm.

You have heard this tale of grief,
O fair daughter of the isles! Rivine was
fair as yourself: shed on her grave a tear.

10

It is night; and I am alone, forlorn
on the hill of storms. The wind is
heard in the mountain. The torrent
shrieks down the rock. No hut receives
me from the rain; forlorn on the hill of winds.

Rise, moon! from behind your
clouds; stars of the night, appear!
Lead me, some light, to the place where
my love rests from the toil of the chase!
his bow near him, unstrung; his dogs
panting around him. But here I must
sit alone, by the rock of the mossy
stream. The stream and the wind
roar; nor can I hear the voice of my love.

Why delay my Shalgar, why the
son of the hill, his promise? Here is
the rock; and the tree; and here the
roaring stream. You promised with
night to be here. Ah! where is my
Shalgar gone? With you I would fly
my father; with you, my brother of
pride. Our race have long been foes;
but we are not foes, O Shalgar!

Cease a little while, O wind! stream,
be you silent a while! let my voice be
heard over the heath; let my wanderer
hear me. Shalgar! it is I who call. Here
is the tree, and the rock. Shalgar, my
love! I am here. Why delay you
your coming? Alas! no answer.

Lo! the moon appears. The
flood is bright in the vale. The rocks
are grey on the face of the hill. But
I see him not on the brow; his dogs
before him tell not that he is coming.
Here I must sit alone.

But who are these that lie beyond
me on the heath? Are they my love
and my brother?—Speak to me, O my
friends! they answer not. My soul is
tormented with fears.—Ah! they are
dead. Their swords are red from the
fight. O my brother! my brother!
Why have you slain my Shalgar? Why,
O Shalgar! have you slain my brother?
Dear were you both to me! Speak to me;
hear my voice, sons of my love! But
alas! they are silent; silent for ever!
Cold are their breasts of clay!

Oh! from the rock of the hill;
from the top of the mountain of winds,
speak you ghosts of the dead! speak,
and I will not be afraid.—Where
are you gone to rest? In what cave of
the hill shall I find you?

I sit in my grief. I wait for morning in my tears. Rear the tomb, you friends of the dead; but close it not till I come. My life flies away like a dream: why should I stay behind? Here shall I rest with my friends by the stream of the founding rock. When night comes on the hill, when the wind is upon the heath; my ghost shall stand in the wind, and mourn the death of my friends. The hunter shall hear from his booth. He shall fear, but love my voice. For sweet shall my voice be for my friends; for pleasant were they both to me.

11

Sad! I am sad indeed: nor small my
cause of woe!—Kirmor, you have
lost no son; you have lost no daughter
of beauty. Connar the valiant lives;
and Annir the fairest of maids. The
boughs of your family flourish, O Kirmor!
but Armyn is the last of his race.

Rise, winds of autumn, rise; blow
upon the dark heath! streams of the
mountains, roar! howl, you tempests,
in the trees! walk through broken
clouds, O moon! show by intervals your
pale face! bring to my mind that sad
night, when all my children fell; when
Arindel the mighty fell; when Daura
the lovely died.

Daura, my daughter! you were
fair; fair as the moon on the hills of
Jura; white as the driven snow; sweet as
the breathing gale. Armour renowned in
war came, and fought Daura's love; he
was not long denied; fair was the hope
of their friends.

Earch son of Odgal repined; for
his brother was slain by Armour. He
came disguised like a son of the sea:
fair was his skiff on the wave; white
his locks of age; calm his serious brow.
"Fairest of women," he said, "lovely daughter
of Armyn! A rock not distant in
the sea, bears a tree on its side; red
shines the fruit afar. There Armour
waits for Daura. I came to fetch
his love. Come, fair daughter of Armyn!"

She went; and she called on Armour.
Nought answered, but the son of the
rock. "Armour, my love! my love!
Why torment you me with fear?
Come, graceful son of Arduart, come;
it is Daura who calls you!"—Earch
the traitor fled laughing to the land.
She lifted up her voice, and cried for
her brother and her father. "Arindel!
Armyn! none to relieve your Daura?"

Her voice came over the sea. Arindel
my son descended from the hill;
rough in the spoils of the chase. His
arrows rattled by his side; his bow was
in his hand; five grey dogs attended
his steps. He saw fierce Earch on the
shore; he seized and bound him to an
oak. Thick fly the thongs of the hide
around his limbs; he loads the wind
with his groans.

Arindel ascends the surgy deep in
his boat, to bring Daura to the land.
Armour came in his wrath, and let fly
the grey-feathered shaft. It sung; it
sunk in your heart, O Arindel my son!
for Earch the traitor you died. What
is your grief, O Daura, when round
your feet is poured your brother's blood!

The boat is broken in two by the
waves. Armor plunges into the sea, to
rescue his Daura or die. Sudden a blast
from the hill comes over the waves.
He sank, and he rose no more.

Alone, on the sea-beat rock, my
daughter was heard to complain. Frequent
and loud were her cries; nor
could her father relieve her. All
night I stood on the shore. All night I
heard her cries. Loud was the wind;
and the rain beat hard on the side of the
mountain. Before morning appeared,
her voice was weak. It died away, like
the evening-breeze among the grass of
the rocks. Spent with grief she expired.
O lay me soon by her side.

When the storms of the mountain
come, when the north lifts the waves
on high, I sit by the sounding shore,
and look on the fatal rock. Often by
the setting moon I see the ghosts of
my children. Indistinct, they walk in

mournful conference together. Will none of you speak to me?—But they do not regard their father.

1

Ryno and Alpin

Ryno. The wind and the rain are over:
calm is the noon of day. The
clouds are divided in heaven. Over
the green hills flies the inconstant sun.
Red through the stony vale comes
down the stream of the hill. Sweet are
your murmurs, O stream! but more
sweet is the voice I hear. It is the voice
of Alpin the son of the song, mourning
for the dead. Bent is his head of age,
and red his tearful eye. Alpin, you
son of the song, why alone on the silent
hill? why complain you, as a
blast in the wood; as a wave on the
lonely shore?

Alpin. My tears, O Ryno! are for the dead;
my voice, for the inhabitants of the
grave. Tall you are on the hill; fair
among the sons of the plain. But you
shall fall like Morar; and the mourner

34

shall sit on your tomb. The hills shall know you no more; your bow shall lie in the hall, unstrung.

You were swift, O Morar! as a doe on the hill; terrible as a meteor of fire. Your wrath was as the storm of December. Your sword in battle, as lightning in the field. Your voice was like a stream after rain; like thunder on distant hills. Many fell by your arm; they were consumed in the flames of your wrath.

But when you returned from war, how peaceful was your brow! Your face was like the sun after rain; like the moon in the silence of night; calm as the breast of the lake when the loud wind is laid.

Narrow is your dwelling now; dark the place of your abode. With three steps I compass your grave, O you who were so great before! Four stones with their heads of moss are the only memorial of you. A tree with scarce a leaf, long grass which whistles in the wind, mark to the hunter's eye the grave of the mighty Morar. Morar! You are low indeed. You have no mother to mourn you; no maid with her tears of love. Dead is she that brought you forth. Fallen is the daughter of Morglan.

Who on his staff is this? Who is this,
whose head is white with age, whose
eyes are red with tears, who quakes
at every step?—It is your father, O
Morar! the father of none but you.
He heard of your fame in battle; he heard
of foes dispersed. He heard of Morar's
fame; why did he not hear of his
wound? Weep, you father of Morar!
weep; but your son hears you not.
Deep is the sleep of the dead; low their
pillow of dust. No more shall he hear
your voice; no more shall he awake at
your call. When shall it be morn in the
grave, to bid the slumberer awake?

Farewell, you bravest of men!
you conqueror in the field! but the field
shall see you no more; nor the dark
wood be lightened with the splendor of
your steel. You have left no son.
But the song shall preserve your name.
Future times shall hear of you; they
shall hear of the fallen Morar.

13

Cuchlaid sat by the wall; by the
tree of the rustling leaf.

His spear leaned against the mossy rock.
His shield lay by him on the grass.
While he thought on the mighty Carbre
whom he slew in battle, the scout of
the ocean came, Moran the son of Fithil.

Rise, Cuchulaid, rise! I see the ships
of Garve. Many are the foe, Cuchulaid;
many the sons of Lochlyn.

Moran! you ever tremble; your
fears increase the foe. They are the
ships of the desert of hills arrived
to assist Cuchulaid.

"I saw their chief," says Moran, "tall as
a rock of ice. His spear is like that fir;
his shield like the rising moon." He sat
upon a rock on the shore, as a grey
cloud upon the hill. "Many, mighty
man!" I said, "many are our heroes;
Garve, well are you named,
many are the sons of our king."

He answered like a wave on the
rock, "Who is like me here? The valiant
live not with me; they go to the
earth from my hand. The king of the
Desert of hills alone can fight with
Garve. Once we wrestled on the hill.
Our heels overturned the wood. Rocks
fell from their place, and rivulets changed
their course. Three days we strove
together; heroes stood at a distance,
and feared. On the fourth, the King
said that I fell; but Garve said, he
stood. Let Cuchulaid yield to him that
is strong as a storm."

"No. I will never yield to man.
Cuchulaid will conquer or die. Go,
Moran, take my spear; strike the shield
of Caithbait which hangs before the
gate. It never rings in peace. My heroes
shall hear on the hill."—

14

Duchommar and Morna

D uchommar. Morna, you fairest of women,
daughter of Cormac-Carbre!
why in the circle of stones, in the cave
of the rock, alone? The stream murmurs
hoarsely. The blast groans
in the aged tree. The lake is troubled
before you. Dark are the clouds of
the sky. But you are like snow on
the heath. Your hair like a thin cloud
of gold on the top of Cromleach. Your
breasts like two smooth rocks on the hill
which is seen from the stream of Brannuin.
Your arms, as two white pillars
in the hall of Fingal.

Morna. Whence the son of Mugruch, Duchommar
the most gloomy of men? Dark
are your brows of terror. Red your rolling
eyes. Does Garve appear on the
sea? What of the foe, Duchommar?

Duchommar. From the hill I return, O Morna, from the hill of the flying deer. Three have I slain with my bow; three with my panting dogs. Daughter of Cormac-Carbre, I love you as my soul. I have slain a deer for you. High was his branchy head; and fleet his feet of wind.

Morna. Gloomy son of Mugruch, Duchommar! I love you not: hard is your heart of rock; dark your terrible brow. But Cadmor the son of Tarman, you are the love of Morna! you are like a sunbeam on the hill, in the day of the gloomy storm. Saw you the son of Tarman, lovely on the hill of the chase? Here the daughter of Cormac-Carbre waits the coming of Cadmor.

Duchommar. And long shall Morna wait. His blood is on my sword. I met him by the mossy stone, by the oak of the noisy stream. He fought; but I slew him; his blood is on my sword. High on the hill I will raise his tomb, daughter of Cormac-Carbre. But love you the son of Mugruch; his arm is strong as a storm.

Morna. And is the son of Tarman fallen? The youth with the breast of snow! The first in the chase of the hill; the foe of the sons of the ocean!—Duchommar, you are gloomy indeed; cruel is

your arm to me.—But give me that
sword, son of Mugruch; I love the
blood of Cadmor.

(*When he hands her the sword,
she quickly stabs him.*)

Duchommar. Daughter of Cormac-Carbre, you
have pierced Duchommar! The sword is
cold in my breast; you have killed the
son of Mugruch. Give me to Moinic
the maid; for much she loved Duchommar.
My tomb she will raise on the
hill; the hunter shall see it, and praise
me.—But draw the sword from my
side, Morna; I feel it cold.—

(*As she comes near, he stabs her. Falling, she
snatches a rock from the cave wall, to place
between them, so that his blood might not
mingle with hers.*)

15

Where is Gealchossa my love, the
daughter of Tuathal-Teachvar?
I left her in the hall of the plain, when I
fought with the hairy Ulfadha. "Return
soon," she said, "O Lamderg!" For
here I wait in sorrow. Her white breast
rose with sighs; her cheek was wet
with tears. But she comes not to meet
Lamderg; or soothe his soul after battle.
Silent is the hall of joy; I hear not
the voice of the singer. Brann does
not shake his chains at the gate, glad
at the coming of his master. Where
is Gealchossa my love, the daughter of
Tuathal-Teachvar?

"Lamderg!" says Firchios son of Aydon,
"Gealchossa may be on the hill;
she and her chosen maids pursuing the
flying deer."

Firchios! no noise I hear. No
sound in the wood of the hill. No
deer fly in my sight; no panting dog
pursues. I see not Gealchossa my

love; fair as the full moon setting on
the hills of Cromleach. Go, Firchios!
go to Allad, the grey-haired son of
the rock. He lives in the circle of
stones; he may tell of Gealchossa.

"Allad!" says Firchios, "you who
dwell in the rock; you who tremble
alone; what saw your eyes of age?"

"I saw," answered Allad the old,
"Ullin the son of Carbre: He came like a
cloud from the hill; he hummed a surly
song as he came, like a storm in
leafless wood. He entered the hall of
the plain. 'Lamderg,' he cried, 'most
dreadful of men! fight, or yield to Ullin.'
'Lamderg,' replied Gealchoffa,
'Lamderg is not here: he fights the
hairy Ulfadha; mighty man, he is not
here. But Lamderg never yields; he
will fight the son of Carbre.' 'Lovely are
you, O daughter of Tuathal-Teachvar!'
said Ullin. 'I carry you to the
house of Carbre; the valiant shall have
Gealchossa. Three days from the top
of Cromleach will I call Lamderg to
fight. The fourth, you belong to Ullin,
if Lamderg die, or fly my sword.' "

"Allad! peace to your dreams!—Sound
the horn, Firchios!—Ullin may
hear, and meet me on the top of Cromleach."

Lamderg rushed on like a storm.
On his spear he leaped over rivers. Few
were his strides up the hill. The rocks
fly back from his heels; loud crashing
they bound to the plain. His armor,
his buckler rang. He hummed a surly
song, like the noise of the falling
stream. Dark as a cloud he stood above;
his arms, like meteors, shone.
From the summit of the hill, he rolled
a rock. Ullin heard in the hall of
Carbre.—

(*text broken off*)

26740065R00028

Printed in Great Britain
by Amazon